Eyes in the Sky: The Role of Technology and Surveillance in the Hunt for bin Laden

Copyright Page

TITLE: Eyes in the Sky: The Role of Technology and Surveillance in the Hunt for bin Laden

1ST Edition

Table of Contents

Eyes sin the Sky: The Role of Technology and Surveillance in the Hunt for bin Laden 1

Chapter 1: Intelligence gathering and analysis during Operation Neptune Spear 5

Chapter 2: Tactical planning and execution of Operation Neptune Spear 12

Chapter 3: Navy SEALs' role in the killing of Osama bin Laden 20

Chapter 4: Impact and aftermath of bin Laden's death on global terrorism 28

Chapter 5: Political implications and reactions to bin Laden's killing.. 36

Chapter 6: The role of technology and surveillance in locating bin Laden 43

Chapter 7: Psychological profiling and understanding of bin Laden as a terrorist leader 51

Chapter 8: The role of international cooperation and intelligence sharing in Operation Neptune Spear 58

Chapter 9: Controversies and conspiracy theories surrounding bin Laden's death 65

Chapter 10: Lessons learned from Operation Neptune Spear for future counterterrorism operations 72

Eyes in the Sky: The Role of Technology and Surveillance in the Hunt for bin Laden

By Roberto Miguel Rodriguez

Book Outline

Introduction:

- Setting the stage: The historical context of the hunt for bin Laden

- The significance of technology and surveillance in the modern intelligence landscape

- The objective of the book: To analyze the various aspects of Operation Neptune Spear and its impact on global terrorism

Intelligence gathering and analysis during Operation Neptune Spear

- The role of intelligence agencies in tracking bin Laden's movements

- Covert operations and undercover agents

- Analyzing intercepted communications and data collection

- Challenges and breakthroughs in deciphering bin Laden's network

Tactical planning and execution of Operation Neptune Spear

- The covert nature of the operation and the need for secrecy

- Preparing for the raid: Training, simulations, and logistics

- Selection and composition of the SEAL team

- The decision-making process and risk assessment

- The raid on the compound: Execution and unexpected challenges

Navy SEALs' role in the killing of Osama bin Laden

- The training and expertise of Navy SEALs

- The mission and objectives of the SEAL team during the raid

- The intense firefight and the capture of bin Laden

- The aftermath: Evaluating the SEALs' performance and lessons learned

Impact and aftermath of bin Laden's death on global terrorism

- The immediate effects on al-Qaeda and affiliated groups

- The symbolic significance of bin Laden's death

- The emergence of new terrorist leaders and organizations

- Counterterrorism efforts post-bin Laden: Successes and challenges

Political implications and reactions to bin Laden's killing

- The response of the United States government and its allies

- Public opinion and international perception of the raid

- Political consequences and implications for the Obama administration

- Debates over the legality and morality of targeted killings

The role of technology and surveillance in locating bin Laden

- Advanced surveillance techniques used in the hunt for bin Laden

- The importance of drones, satellites, and other aerial assets

- The role of data analysis, facial recognition, and other technological advancements

- Ethical considerations and privacy concerns surrounding surveillance

Psychological profiling and understanding of bin Laden as a terrorist leader

- Analyzing bin Laden's ideology and motivations

- The psychology behind his leadership style and influence

- Counterterrorism efforts to understand and combat extremist ideologies

- The legacy of bin Laden as a symbol of global terrorism

The role of international cooperation and intelligence sharing in Operation Neptune Spear

- Collaboration between intelligence agencies and foreign governments

- Challenges and benefits of sharing classified information

- The role of diplomatic efforts and negotiations in the operation's success

- Lessons learned from international cooperation for future counterterrorism operations

Controversies and conspiracy theories surrounding bin Laden's death

- Examining conspiracy theories and alternative narratives

- Addressing skepticism and debunking misinformation

- The role of media and public opinion in shaping conspiracy theories

- Implications for trust in government and intelligence agencies

Lessons learned from Operation Neptune Spear for future counterterrorism operations

- Evaluating the successes and failures of the operation

- Identifying key takeaways for future missions and intelligence efforts

- The evolving nature of counterterrorism and the need for adaptability

- Recommendations for improving intelligence gathering and execution strategies

Conclusion:

- Reflecting on the significance of Operation Neptune Spear in the fight against global terrorism

- The ongoing challenges and complexities of intelligence gathering and analysis

- The role of technology and surveillance in shaping the future of counterterrorism efforts

Chapter 1: Intelligence gathering and analysis during Operation Neptune Spear

The intelligence network and sources

In the thrilling and meticulously researched book, "Eyes in the Sky: The Role of Technology and Surveillance in the Hunt for bin Laden," historians and enthusiasts of intelligence gathering and analysis during Operation Neptune Spear will find a captivating exploration of the methods, sources, and challenges faced by the intelligence community in their pursuit of the world's most wanted terrorist.

The subchapter titled "The intelligence network and sources" delves into the intricate web of intelligence agencies, their collaborations, and the invaluable sources that contributed to the success of Operation Neptune Spear. This operation, which ultimately led to the demise of Osama bin Laden, was a turning point in the fight against global terrorism.

From the CIA's extensive human intelligence network to the cutting-edge technological advancements in signals intelligence, the book provides a comprehensive overview of the various intelligence sources exploited during the operation. Historians will gain insights into the role of informants, electronic intercepts, and satellite imagery, painting a vivid picture of the complexity and sophistication of modern intelligence operations.

Furthermore, the subchapter sheds light on the challenges faced by intelligence analysts as they sifted through mountains of information to identify and locate bin Laden. It explores the difficulties of verifying sources, handling misinformation, and the constant need for corroboration to ensure the reliability of intelligence.

Readers will also gain a deep understanding of the importance of international cooperation and intelligence sharing in Operation Neptune Spear. The book explores the delicate balance between safeguarding sensitive intelligence and building relationships with foreign partners, highlighting the pivotal contributions made by agencies such as the ISI, MI6, and Mossad.

As historians delve into the intelligence network and sources, they will find an objective analysis of the controversies and conspiracy theories surrounding bin Laden's death. The author critically examines these claims, providing a balanced perspective on the operation's outcome and addressing the lingering doubts that persist.

Ultimately, this subchapter offers valuable lessons learned from Operation Neptune Spear for future counterterrorism operations. It underscores the importance of integrating intelligence from various sources, fostering international cooperation, and adapting to emerging technologies. Historians, intelligence professionals, and enthusiasts alike will find "The intelligence network and sources" to be an indispensable resource for understanding the complex world of intelligence gathering and analysis in the pursuit of global security.

Surveillance techniques utilized

In the riveting account of the hunt for Osama bin Laden, "Eyes in the Sky: The Role of Technology and Surveillance in the Hunt for bin Laden," readers are granted unprecedented access to the intricate web of surveillance techniques employed during Operation Neptune Spear. This subchapter delves into the immense efforts undertaken by intelligence agencies and their partners to track down the world's most wanted terrorist.

From the onset, it becomes evident that surveillance played a pivotal role in the success of Operation Neptune Spear. Through a combination of advanced technology, human intelligence, and international cooperation, intelligence agencies painstakingly collected and analyzed vast amounts of data to piece together bin Laden's whereabouts.

Cutting-edge satellite imagery, unmanned aerial vehicles (UAVs), and other high-tech tools formed the backbone of the surveillance efforts. These eyes in the sky provided real-time intelligence, enabling the tactical planning and execution of the operation with unparalleled precision. Such technologies allowed the Navy SEALs to meticulously map out their approach, ensuring minimal casualties and maximum effectiveness.

However, it was not just technology that propelled the hunt for bin Laden forward. Intelligence gathering and analysis played a crucial role in identifying key individuals, tracking their movements, and establishing patterns of behavior. Psychological profiling and an in-depth understanding of bin Laden as a terrorist leader helped shape the surveillance strategies and ultimately led to his location.

International cooperation and intelligence sharing were also instrumental in Operation Neptune Spear. The collaboration between various intelligence agencies, including those from the United States and its allies, allowed for the pooling of resources, expertise, and information. This global effort demonstrated the power of collective intelligence in combating terrorism.

The subchapter also delves into the controversies and conspiracy theories surrounding bin Laden's death. While the official narrative presents a clear picture of a successful mission, alternative interpretations have emerged, questioning the authenticity of the operation. These controversies highlight the complex nature of intelligence operations and the challenges of maintaining transparency in matters of national security.

Ultimately, the successful killing of Osama bin Laden had far-reaching implications. It sent shockwaves through the global terrorism landscape, severely impacting the organizational structure of al-Qaeda and inspiring new counterterrorism initiatives worldwide. Politically, the operation had profound implications, with leaders and governments reacting in different ways to this historic event.

As historians, it is crucial to understand the lessons learned from Operation Neptune Spear. The book provides valuable insights into the importance of technology and surveillance in modern counterterrorism operations. It underscores the significance of international collaboration, as well as the complexities and controversies that surround such high-stakes missions. Through an in-depth analysis of these surveillance techniques, historians can gain a deeper understanding of the multifaceted nature of intelligence gathering and its role in shaping the course of history.

Analyzing the gathered intelligence

In the subchapter titled "Analyzing the gathered intelligence" in the book "Eyes in the Sky: The Role of Technology and Surveillance in the Hunt for bin Laden," we delve into the crucial phase of Operation Neptune Spear - the analysis of the intelligence gathered regarding Osama bin Laden's whereabouts. Historians and experts in the field of intelligence gathering and analysis during this operation will find this subchapter particularly enlightening.

The success of Operation Neptune Spear, the mission that ultimately led to the killing of Osama bin Laden, heavily relied on the meticulous analysis of the gathered intelligence. This subchapter explores the various sources of intelligence and the methods employed to evaluate their credibility. It discusses the role of technology and surveillance in providing critical information, such as satellite imagery, intercepted communications, and human intelligence sources.

Moreover, the subchapter delves into the tactics employed by intelligence analysts to piece together the puzzle of bin Laden's location. It examines how the analysts utilized various analytical techniques, including pattern recognition, link analysis, and geospatial mapping, to identify the compound in Abbottabad where bin Laden was hiding. The subchapter also highlights the challenges faced by the analysts and the uncertainties they encountered during the process.

Additionally, this subchapter emphasizes the importance of international cooperation and intelligence sharing in Operation Neptune Spear. It explores how intelligence agencies from different countries collaborated and shared vital information, enabling a more comprehensive analysis and a more accurate assessment of bin Laden's whereabouts.

Furthermore, the subchapter addresses controversies and conspiracy theories surrounding bin Laden's death. It critically examines these claims and provides evidence-based refutations, highlighting the rigorous analysis conducted by the intelligence community to confirm bin Laden's presence in the compound.

Ultimately, this subchapter concludes with the lessons learned from Operation Neptune Spear for future counterterrorism operations. It highlights the significance of integrating advanced technology and surveillance capabilities with robust intelligence analysis. It also underscores the importance of international collaboration and the need for continuous adaptation and improvement in intelligence gathering and analysis techniques.

In conclusion, the subchapter "Analyzing the gathered intelligence" provides historians and experts in intelligence gathering and analysis with a comprehensive understanding of the critical role played by intelligence analysts during Operation Neptune Spear. It explores the methods, challenges, and successes of analyzing the gathered intelligence, while addressing controversies and drawing valuable lessons for future counterterrorism operations.

Challenges faced in intelligence gathering

In the pursuit of global security, intelligence gathering plays a pivotal role. However, the process of gathering intelligence is not without its challenges. Operation Neptune Spear, the mission that led to the killing of Osama bin Laden, was no exception. This subchapter delves into the various challenges faced during the intelligence gathering phase of Operation Neptune Spear.

One of the primary challenges was the scarcity of credible information on bin Laden's whereabouts. Despite being the mastermind behind the 9/11 attacks, bin Laden had managed to evade capture for nearly a decade. This lack of reliable intelligence posed a significant hurdle for the intelligence community and the Navy SEALs tasked with finding and eliminating him.

Furthermore, the remote and rugged terrain of the Abbottabad compound where bin Laden was hiding added to the difficulties. The compound was fortified with high walls and barbed wire, making it nearly impenetrable. This forced intelligence agencies to rely heavily on advanced surveillance technologies to gather information covertly.

Another challenge was the need to maintain secrecy and operational security. Any leak or compromise of information could jeopardize the entire mission and put the lives of those involved at risk. This necessitated a high level of coordination and trust among the intelligence agencies and the Navy SEALs.

Moreover, the complex web of international politics and intelligence sharing posed additional challenges. Operation Neptune Spear required close collaboration and sharing of intelligence among various nations to gather a comprehensive picture of bin Laden's whereabouts.

Coordinating efforts and ensuring timely and accurate information exchange among different intelligence agencies was no small feat.

Lastly, the psychological profiling and understanding of bin Laden as a terrorist leader proved to be a challenge. Unraveling his mindset, motivations, and decision-making processes was crucial in devising an effective plan to neutralize him. This required extensive analysis of his previous actions, statements, and ideological beliefs.

Despite these challenges, the intelligence community, with the aid of advanced surveillance technologies, successfully gathered the necessary information to execute Operation Neptune Spear. The lessons learned from this operation would go on to shape future counterterrorism operations, emphasizing the importance of technological advancements, international cooperation, and meticulous planning.

In conclusion, intelligence gathering is a multifaceted and intricate process that presents numerous challenges. Operation Neptune Spear, in its pursuit of bin Laden, encountered obstacles such as the scarcity of credible information, the rugged terrain of the hiding location, the need for secrecy, international politics, and understanding the mindset of the target. Overcoming these challenges required a combination of advanced technology, international collaboration, and meticulous analysis. The successful execution of Operation Neptune Spear demonstrated the capabilities of intelligence gathering and its pivotal role in combating global terrorism.

Chapter 2: Tactical planning and execution of Operation Neptune Spear

Formation of the task force

In the subchapter "Formation of the Task Force," we delve into the crucial early stages of Operation Neptune Spear, the mission that ultimately led to the demise of Osama bin Laden. This subchapter explores the meticulous planning and coordination required to assemble a highly skilled and specialized team capable of executing such a high-stakes operation.

Operation Neptune Spear was a multi-agency effort, drawing upon the expertise and resources of various intelligence agencies, military branches, and international partners. The task force responsible for carrying out this historic mission was formed as a result of comprehensive intelligence gathering and analysis, which identified bin Laden's likely location in Abbottabad, Pakistan.

The formation of the task force involved extensive collaboration among intelligence agencies, including the CIA, NSA, and military intelligence units. These agencies pooled their resources, shared vital information, and analyzed data meticulously to ensure the success of the mission. The task force members were carefully selected based on their specific skills, experience, and training, with a focus on executing precision operations in hostile environments.

The Navy SEALs played a central role in the task force, given their expertise in covert operations and counterterrorism. Their selection was based on their exceptional physical fitness, combat experience, and ability to adapt to rapidly changing situations. These elite warriors underwent rigorous training and preparation to ensure they were fully equipped to execute the mission flawlessly.

The subchapter also explores the role of technology and surveillance in locating bin Laden. Advanced surveillance techniques, including satellite imagery, aerial reconnaissance, and electronic communications intercepts, were instrumental in narrowing down the search area. The integration of these technological advancements with human intelligence provided critical insights and actionable intelligence, enabling the task force to plan and execute the operation with precision.

The formation of the task force was not without its challenges and controversies. The subchapter delves into the complexities of international cooperation and intelligence sharing, highlighting the diplomatic and political hurdles that had to be overcome to ensure a unified effort. It also addresses the controversies and conspiracy theories surrounding bin Laden's death, shedding light on the meticulous planning and execution that dispelled doubts and confirmed his demise.

"Formation of the Task Force" serves as a valuable resource for historians and specialists interested in understanding the intricate process of intelligence gathering, tactical planning, and execution of Operation Neptune Spear. It provides insights into the lessons learned from this landmark counterterrorism operation, which continue to shape future efforts in combating global terrorism.

Strategy development for the operation

The successful execution of Operation Neptune Spear, which resulted in the killing of Osama bin Laden, was a result of careful strategy development that encompassed various aspects of intelligence gathering, tactical planning, and execution. This subchapter delves into the intricacies of strategy development for the operation, shedding light on the decisions and considerations that shaped its outcome.

From the outset, the operation required a comprehensive understanding of bin Laden's whereabouts and the surrounding area. Intelligence gathering played a pivotal role in this process. Historians interested in intelligence analysis during this operation will find valuable insights into the techniques employed, including signal intelligence, human intelligence, and imagery intelligence. These sources provided crucial information on bin Laden's location, the layout of the compound in Abbottabad, and the potential threats and challenges faced by the Navy SEALs.

Tactical planning and execution were equally significant components of the operation's strategy. Special emphasis was placed on developing a plan that balanced minimizing civilian casualties with ensuring the success of the mission. Historians studying the tactical aspects of Operation Neptune Spear will gain a deeper understanding of the meticulous planning involved, including the selection of the Navy SEAL team, the use of stealth helicopters, and the coordination of ground and air assets to neutralize any potential threats.

The Navy SEALs' role in the killing of Osama bin Laden cannot be understated. This subchapter explores their training, preparation, and execution of the mission, highlighting the bravery and professionalism that characterized their actions. It also examines the challenges they faced during the operation and the lessons learned from their experiences.

Furthermore, the subchapter analyzes the impact and aftermath of bin Laden's death on global terrorism. It delves into the subsequent shifts in terrorist tactics and strategies, as well as the implications for counterterrorism efforts worldwide. The political implications and reactions to bin Laden's killing are also examined, providing historians with a comprehensive understanding of the event's broader significance.

Lastly, the subchapter addresses the controversies and conspiracy theories surrounding bin Laden's death, providing an objective analysis of the evidence and offering insights into the reasons behind the skepticism. It concludes with a discussion on the lessons learned from Operation Neptune Spear and their implications for future counterterrorism operations, emphasizing the importance of intelligence sharing, international cooperation, and the effective use of technology and surveillance.

In conclusion, this subchapter provides historians with an in-depth exploration of the strategy development for Operation Neptune Spear. By examining the intelligence gathering, tactical planning, and execution, it offers valuable insights into the various facets that contributed to the successful operation, shedding light on the lessons learned and their implications for future counterterrorism endeavors.

Coordinating with different units and agencies

In the pursuit of Osama bin Laden, one of the most wanted terrorists in history, the successful execution of Operation Neptune Spear required seamless coordination among various units and agencies. This subchapter explores the vital role played by intelligence gathering and analysis, tactical planning and execution, and international cooperation in this historic mission.

From the outset, it was evident that capturing or killing bin Laden would necessitate gathering and analyzing intelligence from multiple sources. Historically, intelligence agencies had struggled to piece together fragmented information, but Operation Neptune Spear was different. It brought together intelligence from both human sources on the ground and advanced technological surveillance systems, enabling a comprehensive understanding of bin Laden's network.

Tactical planning and execution were paramount in ensuring the success of the mission. Navy SEALs, renowned for their expertise in special operations, were selected for this high-stakes mission. Their role in the killing of bin Laden exemplified their exceptional training, precision, and bravery. The subchapter delves into the meticulous planning that went into the operation and the daring execution that ultimately led to bin Laden's demise.

International cooperation and intelligence sharing played a crucial role in Operation Neptune Spear. The hunt for bin Laden required collaboration between intelligence agencies from various countries, who shared intelligence, resources, and expertise. This unprecedented level of cooperation highlighted the global commitment to eradicating terrorism and showcased the power of collective action.

However, the impact and aftermath of bin Laden's death on global terrorism were complex and multifaceted. This subchapter examines the short-term disruption caused to al-Qaeda's operations and the subsequent rise of splinter groups. It also explores the continued threat posed by global terrorism and the need for sustained efforts to counter it.

The political implications and reactions to bin Laden's killing are also explored, including the immediate responses from world leaders and the subsequent debates over its legality. Furthermore, the subchapter delves into the controversies and conspiracy theories surrounding bin Laden's death, providing an objective analysis of the evidence and debunking unfounded claims.

Lastly, this subchapter draws lessons from Operation Neptune Spear that are applicable to future counterterrorism operations. It highlights the importance of advanced technology and surveillance in locating high-value targets, the significance of international cooperation, and the need for continuous adaptation in the face of evolving terrorist threats.

Overall, "Coordinating with different units and agencies" sheds light on the intricate web of intelligence gathering, tactical planning, international cooperation, and the challenges faced in the execution of

Operation Neptune Spear. Historians and those interested in intelligence analysis, tactical operations, and counterterrorism will gain valuable insights into this landmark mission and its far-reaching implications.

Execution of the operation

The execution of Operation Neptune Spear was a culmination of meticulous intelligence gathering and analysis, tactical planning, and the deployment of highly skilled Navy SEALs. This subchapter delves into the intricacies of the operation, shedding light on the key elements that led to the successful killing of Osama bin Laden.

The operation, carried out on May 2, 2011, was the result of years of intelligence work, including the meticulous tracking and surveillance of bin Laden. Advanced technology and surveillance played a crucial role in locating the elusive terrorist leader. Satellite imagery, signal intelligence, and human intelligence were combined, providing a comprehensive picture of bin Laden's whereabouts.

Tactical planning and execution were vital to ensuring the success of the operation. Navy SEAL Team Six, known for their expertise in covert operations, was selected to carry out the mission. Their training, skills, and experience were crucial in navigating the complex compound in Abbottabad, Pakistan, where bin Laden was hiding.

The role of the Navy SEALs in the killing of bin Laden cannot be overstated. Their bravery and precision allowed them to neutralize the threat swiftly and efficiently, despite facing unexpected resistance. The operation showcased the capabilities of special forces in high-stakes missions and solidified their reputation as an elite fighting force.

The death of bin Laden had a significant impact on global terrorism. It dealt a severe blow to al-Qaeda and sent a clear message that terrorist leaders would not go unpunished. However, it also sparked concerns about potential retaliation and the reorganization of terrorist networks.

The political implications and reactions to bin Laden's killing were far-reaching. The operation was hailed as a major victory for the United States and its allies, boosting public morale and confidence in counterterrorism efforts. However, it also raised questions about the legality of the operation and strained international relations, particularly with Pakistan.

The use of technology and surveillance in locating bin Laden showcased the advancements made in intelligence gathering. From satellite imagery to unmanned aerial vehicles, these tools proved instrumental in tracking down the world's most wanted terrorist.

Psychological profiling and understanding of bin Laden as a terrorist leader were critical in devising strategies to neutralize him. This subchapter explores the motivations, ideologies, and tactics employed by bin Laden, shedding light on the mindset of a terrorist mastermind.

International cooperation and intelligence sharing were vital in the success of Operation Neptune Spear. The operation would not have been possible without the collaboration and support of various intelligence agencies and governments.

Controversies and conspiracy theories surrounding bin Laden's death emerged in the aftermath of the operation. This subchapter delves into these controversies, examining the evidence and providing a balanced analysis of the different narratives.

Finally, the lessons learned from Operation Neptune Spear are crucial for future counterterrorism operations. This subchapter highlights the key takeaways from the operation, including the importance of intelligence sharing, the need for adaptable strategies, and the role of technology in modern warfare.

Overall, the execution of Operation Neptune Spear was a testament to the power of intelligence, technology, and skilled operatives in the fight against terrorism. By exploring the various facets of the operation, this subchapter provides historians and specialists in intelligence gathering, tactical planning, and counterterrorism with a comprehensive understanding of this historic event.

Chapter 3: Navy SEALs' role in the killing of Osama bin Laden

Selection and training of the SEAL team

The successful operation to eliminate Osama bin Laden was a result of meticulous planning, precise execution, and the unparalleled skills of the Navy SEAL team involved. The selection and training process of these elite warriors played a crucial role in ensuring the success of Operation Neptune Spear.

The SEAL team that carried out the mission was handpicked from the United States Navy's Sea, Air, and Land (SEAL) teams, renowned for their exceptional physical and mental capabilities. Candidates undergo a rigorous selection process that tests their endurance, strength, and ability to perform under extreme pressure. Only the best of the best are chosen to become SEALs.

Once selected, the SEAL candidates embark on a grueling training program known as Basic Underwater Demolition/SEAL (BUD/S) training. This six-month-long program pushes candidates to their physical and mental limits, preparing them for the demanding tasks they will face as SEALs. From the treacherous cold waters of the Pacific to the punishing obstacle courses, BUD/S training screens out those who are not fit to become part of this elite force.

After completing BUD/S, candidates move on to the SEAL Qualification Training (SQT), where they acquire specialized skills such as close-quarters combat, marksmanship, and tactical planning. This training ensures that the SEALs are versatile and capable of handling any situation they may encounter during a mission.

The selection and training process of the SEAL team for Operation Neptune Spear was even more rigorous and stringent than usual. The mission required individuals with exceptional combat skills, intelligence, and the ability to work seamlessly as a team. The SEALs chosen for this operation underwent additional training and specialized briefings to familiarize themselves with the specific objectives and challenges they would face.

The selection and training of the SEAL team for Operation Neptune Spear exemplified the dedication and commitment of these elite warriors. Their preparation for this mission was intensive and comprehensive, ensuring that they were equipped with the skills and mindset necessary to complete their mission successfully.

The SEAL team's selection and training process was a critical factor in the ultimate success of Operation Neptune Spear. Their exceptional abilities, honed through rigorous training, allowed them to carry out their mission with precision and effectiveness. The SEALs' role in the killing of Osama bin Laden serves as a testament to the importance of selecting and training the best individuals for high-stakes operations.

In the aftermath of the mission, the selection and training process of the SEALs garnered international attention and admiration. The successful elimination of bin Laden demonstrated the effectiveness of their training and solidified their reputation as the world's premier special operations force.

Infiltration and approach to the target

The successful operation to eliminate Osama bin Laden, known as Operation Neptune Spear, was a culmination of meticulous planning, intelligence gathering, and precise execution. This subchapter delves into the critical aspects of the infiltration and approach to the target, shedding light on the extraordinary efforts undertaken to bring the world's most wanted terrorist to justice.

One of the key elements of Operation Neptune Spear was the tactical planning and execution. The Navy SEALs, renowned for their expertise in covert operations, played a central role in this mission. Their extensive training and combat experience allowed them to navigate the challenging terrain of Abbottabad, Pakistan, with utmost precision and stealth. This subchapter explores the strategies employed by these elite operatives, including the use of advanced weaponry and cutting-edge surveillance technologies to ensure the success of their mission.

The role of technology and surveillance in locating bin Laden cannot be overstated. This subchapter highlights the remarkable advancements in intelligence gathering techniques that enabled the identification of bin Laden's whereabouts. It delves into the sophisticated surveillance systems, including satellite imagery, unmanned aerial vehicles (UAVs), and signal intelligence, that provided vital information about the compound in Abbottabad. The meticulous analysis of this data by intelligence agencies played a pivotal role in the operation's success.

Understanding bin Laden as a terrorist leader required comprehensive psychological profiling. This subchapter explores the exhaustive efforts undertaken by intelligence agencies to gain insights into bin Laden's mindset, motivations, and decision-making processes. By unraveling the complexities of his personality and ideology, analysts were able to anticipate his actions and develop effective strategies to neutralize him.

Operation Neptune Spear was a prime example of the significance of international cooperation and intelligence sharing. This subchapter highlights the collaboration between multiple intelligence agencies, including the Central Intelligence Agency (CIA) and foreign counterparts, to gather and analyze information crucial to the mission's success. It underscores the importance of such cooperation in combating global terrorism and emphasizes the lessons learned for future counterterrorism operations.

The aftermath of bin Laden's death had far-reaching implications on global terrorism and politics. This subchapter explores the impact of his demise on extremist organizations, the subsequent waves of terrorist attacks, and the political reactions from various nations. It also delves into the controversies and conspiracy theories surrounding bin Laden's death, shedding light on the skepticism and speculation that emerged in the aftermath.

In conclusion, the infiltration and approach to the target in Operation Neptune Spear represented a remarkable feat of intelligence gathering, strategic planning, and execution. This subchapter provides historians and experts in intelligence gathering and analysis a comprehensive understanding of the intricacies involved in this historic mission. It serves as a testament to the power of technology, the importance of international cooperation, and the lessons learned for future counterterrorism operations.

The firefight and elimination of bin Laden

In the subchapter titled "The firefight and elimination of bin Laden," we delve into the gripping events that unfolded during Operation Neptune Spear, the mission that ultimately led to the demise of the world's most wanted terrorist, Osama bin Laden. This section of "Eyes in the Sky: The Role of Technology and Surveillance in the Hunt for bin Laden" explores the various aspects of this historic operation, catering specifically to historians and experts in intelligence gathering, tactical planning, and counterterrorism.

As the operation commenced, the tactical planning and execution of Operation Neptune Spear proved to be a testament to the precision and expertise of Navy SEALs. With the help of advanced technology and surveillance, the SEALs meticulously carried out their mission, navigating the compound where bin Laden was hiding. This subchapter sheds light on the meticulous planning and execution strategies employed during this critical phase of the operation.

The Navy SEALs' role in the killing of bin Laden is a focal point of this subchapter. By analyzing their training, tactics, and bravery, we gain a deeper understanding of how these elite forces successfully neutralized the threat posed by bin Laden, a man who had eluded capture for years. Their heroic actions and the risks they undertook are explored in detail, offering invaluable insights into the operation.

The impact and aftermath of bin Laden's death on global terrorism cannot be overstated. This subchapter examines the immediate and long-term consequences of his elimination, including the disruption of Al-Qaeda's leadership structure and the subsequent rise of affiliate groups. It also delves into the political implications and varied reactions to his killing, both domestically and internationally.

Furthermore, this chapter addresses the vital role of technology and surveillance in locating bin Laden. By analyzing the methods employed to track and monitor the terrorist leader, we gain a comprehensive understanding of the cutting-edge technologies utilized during the operation. Additionally, the subchapter explores the psychological profiling and understanding of bin Laden as a terrorist leader, shedding light on the complex motivations and mindset that drove his actions.

The role of international cooperation and intelligence sharing in Operation Neptune Spear is another significant aspect explored in this subchapter. It highlights the collaboration between intelligence agencies from different nations, emphasizing the importance of multinational efforts in combating global terrorism.

Finally, this subchapter delves into the controversies and conspiracy theories surrounding bin Laden's death, offering a balanced analysis of the evidence and debunking unfounded claims. Drawing from the lessons learned during Operation Neptune Spear, it concludes by examining the valuable insights gained and their implications for future counterterrorism operations.

In short, this subchapter provides a comprehensive account of the firefight and elimination of bin Laden, offering historians and experts in intelligence gathering, tactical planning, and counterterrorism a detailed analysis of these pivotal events in modern history.

Extraction and aftermath for the SEAL team

As the culmination of years of intelligence gathering and meticulous planning, Operation Neptune Spear was executed with precision and audacity. At the heart of this historic mission were the brave and elite Navy SEALs, whose role in the killing of Osama bin Laden would forever change the course of global terrorism.

The extraction of the SEAL team from the compound in Abbottabad, Pakistan, where bin Laden had been hiding, was a critical phase of the operation. Under cover of darkness and with the aid of cutting-edge technology and surveillance, the team swiftly and securely made their way to the extraction point. Their successful extraction was a testament to their rigorous training, tactical planning, and unwavering determination.

The aftermath of bin Laden's death reverberated across the globe. The impact on global terrorism was significant, as it dealt a severe blow to al-Qaeda and served as a symbolic victory against extremism. However, it also sparked concerns about potential retaliatory attacks and the possibility of power struggles within the organization.

Politically, bin Laden's killing had far-reaching implications. The United States and its allies celebrated the successful mission, bolstering their stance in the fight against terrorism. However, it also strained diplomatic relationships, particularly with Pakistan, raising questions about their role in harboring the world's most wanted terrorist.

The extraction and aftermath of the SEAL team's operation were not without controversy. Conspiracy theories surrounding bin Laden's death circulated, with skeptics questioning the official narrative. These controversies fueled debates, and the truth became a subject of intense scrutiny.

Operation Neptune Spear also shed light on the importance of international cooperation and intelligence sharing in counterterrorism efforts. The successful mission was the result of collaboration between various intelligence agencies and governments, underscoring the significance of working together to combat a common enemy.

From a psychological perspective, understanding bin Laden as a terrorist leader was crucial in the planning and execution of the operation. Psychological profiling provided insights into his mindset, enabling the SEAL team to anticipate his behavior and react accordingly.

Lessons learned from Operation Neptune Spear have greatly influenced future counterterrorism operations. The successful operation highlighted the need for advanced technology and surveillance capabilities, as well as the importance of meticulous planning and training. It also emphasized the significance of adaptability and flexibility in the face of unforeseen challenges.

In conclusion, the extraction and aftermath of the SEAL team's mission in Operation Neptune Spear showcased the bravery, skill, and dedication of these elite soldiers. Their role in the killing of Osama bin Laden reshaped the fight against global terrorism, sparking political and diplomatic consequences. The operation's success and controversies surrounding bin Laden's death have left lasting lessons for historians and those involved in intelligence gathering and analysis, tactical planning, and future counterterrorism operations.

Chapter 4: Impact and aftermath of bin Laden's death on global terrorism

Disruption of al-Qaeda's leadership

In the subchapter titled "Disruption of al-Qaeda's Leadership," we delve into the pivotal moment when the leadership of the notorious terrorist organization was thrown into disarray. This disruption resulted from the successful operation known as Neptune Spear, which ultimately led to the killing of al-Qaeda's most prominent figurehead, Osama bin Laden. This chapter explores the far-reaching implications of this event and its significance in the global war on terror.

The operation was meticulously planned and executed, with an extensive focus on intelligence gathering and analysis. The book highlights the role of cutting-edge technology and surveillance in locating bin Laden, shedding light on the groundbreaking tools and techniques employed by intelligence agencies. The audience, particularly those interested in intelligence gathering and analysis during Operation Neptune Spear, will gain valuable insights into the advancements that played a vital role in this historic operation.

Furthermore, the subchapter explores the tactical planning and execution of Operation Neptune Spear, considering the Navy SEALs' role in the mission. It unravels the challenges faced by the highly skilled Special Forces unit, their training, and the intricate details of the operation itself. Historians and individuals fascinated by the tactical aspects of military operations will find this section enlightening, as it provides a comprehensive account of the mission's intricacies.

The impact of bin Laden's death on global terrorism is also examined, offering an in-depth analysis of how this event altered the landscape of international security. The book delves into the aftermath of bin Laden's demise, exploring the immediate and long-term consequences it had on al-Qaeda and their operations. The political implications and varied reactions to bin Laden's killing are discussed, providing a comprehensive understanding of the geopolitical ramifications of this event.

Additionally, the subchapter delves into the controversies and conspiracy theories surrounding bin Laden's death. By addressing these controversial aspects, the book ensures a well-rounded exploration of the subject matter, allowing historians to critically analyze the various narratives surrounding this historic event.

Finally, this subchapter draws valuable lessons from Operation Neptune Spear, offering insights into the best practices and strategies for future counterterrorism operations. It emphasizes the importance of international cooperation and intelligence sharing, highlighting the collaborative efforts that were instrumental in the success of this mission.

In conclusion, the subchapter "Disruption of al-Qaeda's Leadership" provides a comprehensive analysis of the events surrounding the killing of Osama bin Laden. With its focus on intelligence gathering, tactical planning, global implications, political reactions, and lessons learned, it caters to historians and individuals interested in various niches such as intelligence, military operations, counterterrorism, and international security.

Repercussions for terrorist networks worldwide

The death of Osama bin Laden had far-reaching repercussions for terrorist networks worldwide, fundamentally altering the landscape of global terrorism. This subchapter explores the profound impact and aftermath of bin Laden's death on terrorist organizations, intelligence agencies, and counterterrorism efforts.

With the demise of their charismatic leader, al-Qaeda and its affiliated groups faced a severe blow to their organizational structure and morale.

Bin Laden had played a pivotal role in inspiring and guiding terrorist activities, providing strategic direction, and attracting new recruits. His death left a void that would be challenging to fill, leading to power struggles and internal conflicts within the network. As a result, al-Qaeda became fragmented, losing its central command structure and struggling to maintain its previous level of operational effectiveness.

Intelligence agencies worldwide seized the opportunity to exploit the chaos within terrorist organizations. The intelligence gathered during Operation Neptune Spear, which led to bin Laden's demise, provided critical insights into al-Qaeda's global network. This information enabled agencies to target and dismantle key operational cells, disrupt communication channels, and apprehend high-value targets. The successful mission demonstrated the importance of intelligence gathering and analysis in unraveling terrorist networks and preventing future attacks.

The tactical planning and execution of Operation Neptune Spear by Navy SEALs showcased the capabilities of special operations forces in conducting complex and high-risk missions. Their role in eliminating bin Laden highlighted the significance of special forces in counterterrorism operations, setting a precedent for future operations targeting high-value individuals.

The political implications and reactions to bin Laden's killing reverberated globally. The United States, in particular, experienced a surge in national pride and a renewed sense of security. However, the death of bin Laden also raised concerns about potential retaliation and increased threats from extremist groups seeking revenge. Governments worldwide had to reassess their counterterrorism strategies and allocate resources accordingly.

The role of technology and surveillance in locating bin Laden demonstrated its indispensable role in modern warfare and intelligence operations. Advanced surveillance technologies, including unmanned aerial vehicles and satellite imagery, played a crucial role in monitoring terrorist activities, identifying targets, and gathering actionable intelligence.

Psychological profiling and understanding of bin Laden as a terrorist leader shed light on the motivations, strategies, and tactics adopted by extremist groups. This knowledge facilitated the development of more effective counterterrorism approaches by focusing on the ideological drivers behind terrorism.

International cooperation and intelligence sharing played a pivotal role in the success of Operation Neptune Spear. The operation highlighted the necessity of collaboration among intelligence agencies, demonstrating the power of shared resources, expertise, and information in disrupting terrorist networks.

Despite the success of Operation Neptune Spear, controversies and conspiracy theories surrounding bin Laden's death emerged. These controversies raised questions about the veracity of the operation and fueled speculation about the US government's role. Such debates underscored the challenges of managing the dissemination of information in the age of mass media and the importance of transparency in counterterrorism operations.

In conclusion, bin Laden's death had significant repercussions for terrorist networks worldwide. It weakened al-Qaeda, disrupted their operational capabilities, and prompted a reassessment of counterterrorism strategies globally. The successful operation highlighted the importance of intelligence gathering, tactical planning, international cooperation, and the role of technology in combating terrorism. However, controversies surrounding bin Laden's death underscored the need for transparency and accurate information dissemination in counterterrorism efforts. The lessons learned from

Operation Neptune Spear continue to shape future counterterrorism operations and inform the fight against global terrorism.

Shifts in terrorist tactics and strategies

The subchapter "Shifts in terrorist tactics and strategies" delves into the changing landscape of terrorism and how it evolved leading up to the operation that ultimately resulted in the death of Osama bin Laden. This section aims to provide historians with a comprehensive understanding of the shifts in tactics and strategies employed by terrorists during this period.

As intelligence gathering and analysis during Operation Neptune Spear played a crucial role in the success of the mission, it is important to examine how terrorist groups adapted in response to increased surveillance and technological advancements. The chapter explores the ways in which terrorists modified their communication methods, recruitment strategies, and operational planning to avoid detection.

Furthermore, the subchapter delves into the tactical planning and execution of Operation Neptune Spear itself. It highlights the meticulous planning and coordination necessary for such a high-stakes mission, emphasizing the role of Navy SEALs in carrying out the operation. This section also provides insights into the unique challenges faced by the SEALs and the innovative tactics employed to overcome them.

The impact and aftermath of bin Laden's death on global terrorism are also examined, shedding light on how the elimination of such a prominent figure affected the structure and dynamics of terrorist organizations worldwide. Historians will gain insights into the response of these groups, the emergence of new leaders, and the potential for retaliatory attacks.

Moreover, the political implications and reactions to bin Laden's killing are explored, analyzing how this event affected international relations and domestic politics. The subchapter also addresses controversies and conspiracy theories surrounding bin Laden's death, offering an objective analysis of these claims and their potential implications.

Lessons learned from Operation Neptune Spear for future counterterrorism operations are discussed, focusing on the significance of technology and surveillance in locating high-value targets. The subchapter highlights the importance of international cooperation and intelligence sharing in the success of such operations, shedding light on the collaborative efforts of various countries in the hunt for bin Laden.

In conclusion, "Shifts in terrorist tactics and strategies" provides historians with a detailed account of the evolving tactics and strategies employed by terrorists leading up to the operation that resulted in the death of Osama bin Laden. It explores the impact of his death on global terrorism, the political implications, and the role of technology and surveillance in counterterrorism operations. This subchapter aims to offer valuable insights for historians, intelligence professionals, and those interested in the complexities of modern terrorism.

The significance of bin Laden's death in the War on Terror

The significance of bin Laden's death in the War on Terror cannot be overstated. It marked a major milestone in the global fight against terrorism and had wide-ranging implications for both the United States and the world.

Operation Neptune Spear, the mission that led to bin Laden's demise, represented the culmination of years of intelligence gathering and analysis. The painstaking work of numerous agencies and analysts was instrumental in locating the terrorist leader. It demonstrated the power of modern technology and surveillance in tracking and monitoring high-value targets. The book "Eyes in the Sky: The Role of Technology and Surveillance in the Hunt for bin Laden" delves into the various methods and techniques employed in this operation.

Tactical planning and execution were key components of Operation Neptune Spear. The Navy SEALs, renowned for their expertise in special operations, played a crucial role in the mission. Their training, skills, and bravery were instrumental in successfully eliminating bin Laden. The book provides an in-depth analysis of the SEALs' involvement and their operational tactics.

The impact of bin Laden's death on global terrorism cannot be underestimated. It dealt a significant blow to al-Qaeda, the extremist group he led. His demise disrupted their chain of command and weakened their influence. However, it also led to a shift in the organization's strategy, with decentralized cells becoming more prevalent. The book explores the immediate aftermath of bin Laden's death and its long-term effects on global terrorism.

Politically, bin Laden's killing had far-reaching implications. It was a major victory for the United States and its allies, bolstering their credibility in the War on Terror. However, it also sparked a wave of conspiracy theories and controversies. The book examines the political reactions to bin Laden's killing and the subsequent debates surrounding the circumstances of his death.

Additionally, the book delves into the psychological profiling and understanding of bin Laden as a terrorist leader. It analyzes his motivations, tactics, and mindset, offering valuable insights into the mind of a terrorist mastermind.

Furthermore, international cooperation and intelligence sharing played a vital role in Operation Neptune Spear. The book explores the collaborative efforts of various intelligence agencies and countries, highlighting the importance of such alliances in combating global terrorism.

Lastly, the book draws lessons from Operation Neptune Spear that can be applied to future counterterrorism operations. It examines the successes and failures of the mission, identifying areas for improvement and offering valuable insights for policymakers, intelligence analysts, and military strategists.

In conclusion, the significance of bin Laden's death in the War on Terror cannot be understated. From the intelligence gathering and analysis to the tactical planning and execution, from the role of the Navy SEALs to the impact on global terrorism, the book "Eyes in the Sky: The Role of Technology and Surveillance in the Hunt for bin Laden" provides a comprehensive exploration of the multifaceted significance of this historic event. Historians and those interested in intelligence gathering, counterterrorism, and global security will find this subchapter invaluable in understanding the complexities of the War on Terror and the role of technology in the fight against terrorism.

Chapter 5: Political implications and reactions to bin Laden's killing

Public response to the news

The news of Osama bin Laden's death spread rapidly throughout the world in the early hours of May 2, 2011. The public response to this significant event was nothing short of extraordinary. People from all corners of the globe, regardless of nationality or political affiliation, were captivated by the news and had varying reactions to the demise of one of the world's most wanted terrorists.

In the United States, the news of bin Laden's death was met with jubilation and relief. The American people had been living under the specter of terrorism since the devastating attacks of September 11, 2001. The successful operation to eliminate bin Laden was seen as a significant achievement in the global war on terror. It was a moment of closure and justice for the victims of 9/11 and their families.

Internationally, the response was mixed. Many countries, particularly those that had been targeted by bin Laden and his Al-Qaeda network, welcomed the news and expressed solidarity with the United States. They saw bin Laden's death as a blow to global terrorism and a step forward in ensuring global security.

However, there were also pockets of skepticism and disbelief. Conspiracy theories suggesting that bin Laden was still alive or that the entire operation was staged began to circulate. These theories gained traction in some parts of the world, fueled by a general mistrust of the United States and its intelligence agencies. Despite overwhelming evidence of bin Laden's death, these conspiracy theories persisted and continue to be debated to this day.

The impact of bin Laden's death on global terrorism cannot be underestimated. While it did not eradicate the threat entirely, it significantly weakened Al-Qaeda and disrupted its leadership structure. It also sent a strong message to other terrorist organizations that the United States and its allies would not rest until those responsible for acts of terror were brought to justice.

From a political standpoint, the news of bin Laden's death had both domestic and international implications. Domestically, it provided a much-needed boost to President Barack Obama's approval ratings and bolstered his image as a strong leader in the fight against terrorism. Internationally, it raised questions about the relationship between the United States and Pakistan, as bin Laden was found hiding in a compound near the Pakistani military academy.

In conclusion, the public response to the news of Osama bin Laden's death was a mix of jubilation, relief, skepticism, and conspiracy theories. It had a profound impact on global terrorism, politics, and the public's perception of the United States' ability to combat terrorism. The ramifications of this historic event continue to shape the way intelligence gathering, surveillance, and counterterrorism operations are conducted today.

International diplomatic fallout

International diplomatic fallout refers to the consequences and repercussions that occur on the diplomatic front following a significant event or action. In the case of the operation to hunt down and kill Osama bin Laden, known as Operation Neptune Spear, there were various international diplomatic fallout that had a lasting impact on global relations, intelligence cooperation, and counterterrorism efforts.

One of the immediate diplomatic fallout of bin Laden's death was the strained relationship between the United States and Pakistan. The fact that bin Laden was found hiding in Abbottabad, a city in Pakistan, raised questions about Pakistan's knowledge and possible involvement in sheltering the world's most wanted terrorist. This led to a deterioration of trust between the two countries and a reevaluation of their bilateral relationship.

Furthermore, the operation also highlighted the complex and delicate nature of international intelligence sharing and cooperation. The successful operation relied heavily on intelligence gathered from multiple countries, including the United States, Pakistan, and other allies. However, the revelation that the United States had conducted a unilateral operation without informing or seeking permission from Pakistan strained relations with other countries and raised concerns about the United States' respect for sovereignty.

The diplomatic fallout extended beyond the immediate aftermath of the operation. It had a lasting impact on global terrorism and counterterrorism efforts. Bin Laden's death created a power vacuum within al-Qaeda, leading to a struggle for leadership and a fragmentation of the organization. This resulted in a shift in global terrorism dynamics, with the rise of new terrorist groups and the decentralization of power within existing ones.

Moreover, the operation also raised questions about the legality and morality of targeted killings, particularly when conducted on foreign soil without the consent of the host country. This sparked debates within the international community and fueled controversies and conspiracy theories surrounding bin Laden's death.

The international diplomatic fallout from Operation Neptune Spear highlighted the complexities and challenges of conducting counterterrorism operations on a global scale. It underscored the importance of international cooperation and intelligence sharing in combating terrorism while also raising concerns about the potential infringements on national sovereignty. The aftermath of bin Laden's death served as a valuable lesson for future counterterrorism operations, emphasizing the need for careful diplomatic maneuvering and a comprehensive understanding of the potential diplomatic fallout that may occur.

Political implications for the United States

The killing of Osama bin Laden on May 2, 2011, had profound political implications for the United States. This historic event marked a significant milestone in the global war on terror and had far-reaching consequences for both domestic and international politics.

First and foremost, bin Laden's death was a major victory for the United States in its fight against terrorism. The successful operation, known as Operation Neptune Spear, served as a testament to the effectiveness of American intelligence gathering and analysis. The meticulous planning and execution of the operation by the Navy SEALs showcased the unparalleled tactical capabilities of the U.S. military.

The political implications of bin Laden's death were not limited to the immediate aftermath. The impact of his demise on global terrorism cannot be overstated. With bin Laden out of the picture, Al-Qaeda, the terrorist organization he led, was left without its charismatic and strategic leader. This created a power vacuum within the group and weakened its operational capacity. However, it also sparked concerns about the rise of other extremist organizations that could potentially fill the void left by bin Laden.

The political reactions to bin Laden's killing were mixed. While the majority of the international community celebrated his death as a significant blow to terrorism, there were some countries and individuals who expressed skepticism and even condemned the operation. This divergence of opinions highlighted the complex nature of global politics and the differing views on counterterrorism strategies.

The role of technology and surveillance in locating bin Laden cannot be overlooked. Eyes in the Sky, such as drones and satellites, played a crucial role in tracking his movements and gathering intelligence. This underscores the importance of technological advancements in modern intelligence operations and their impact on political decision-making.

Moreover, bin Laden's death sparked controversies and conspiracy theories surrounding the circumstances of his demise. Questions regarding the legality of the operation, the Pakistani government's alleged knowledge of his whereabouts, and the disposal of his body fueled public debates and raised concerns about transparency and accountability.

Operation Neptune Spear and its aftermath provided invaluable lessons for future counterterrorism operations. The successful mission highlighted the importance of international cooperation and intelligence sharing in combating terrorism. It also underscored the significance of psychological profiling and understanding terrorist leaders to effectively dismantle their organizations.

In conclusion, the political implications of Osama bin Laden's death were profound for the United States. The operation showcased American intelligence capabilities, weakened Al-Qaeda, and sparked global debates on counterterrorism strategies. The role of technology, international cooperation, and psychological profiling were central to the success of Operation Neptune Spear. However, the controversies and conspiracy theories surrounding bin Laden's death highlighted the challenges and complexities of modern counterterrorism efforts.

The role of bin Laden's death in the 2012 U.S. Presidential election

The death of Osama bin Laden, the notorious leader of al-Qaeda, was a significant event that had far-reaching implications not only in the realm of global terrorism but also in the political landscape of the United States. The 2012 U.S. Presidential election was marked by the resonance of this event, shaping the narrative of national security and counterterrorism efforts.

Bin Laden's death occurred on May 2, 2011, during Operation Neptune Spear, a covert mission carried out by Navy SEALs in Abbottabad, Pakistan. This operation was the culmination of years of intelligence gathering, tactical planning, and international cooperation, underscoring the importance of various aspects of intelligence and counterterrorism efforts.

The successful operation, led by the U.S. military and intelligence agencies, showcased the effectiveness of cutting-edge technology and surveillance in locating and targeting high-value targets like bin Laden. The use of satellite imagery, aerial drones, and other advanced surveillance tools played a critical role in the identification and tracking of bin Laden's compound. This technological prowess not only bolstered the morale of intelligence agencies but also highlighted the significance of continued investment in technology for future counterterrorism operations.

The operation also shed light on the meticulous psychological profile that was developed to understand bin Laden as a terrorist leader. Detailed analysis of his behavior, beliefs, and motivations enabled intelligence agencies to anticipate his movements and exploit his vulnerabilities. This approach to psychological profiling has since become a valuable tool in the understanding of other terrorist leaders, aiding in the identification and neutralization of potential threats to national security.

The impact of bin Laden's death on global terrorism was profound. It sent a clear message that no terrorist leader would be safe from the long arm of justice. The demise of bin Laden dealt a severe blow to al-Qaeda, disrupting its organizational structure and undermining its ability to carry out large-scale attacks. This success also prompted a reevaluation of counterterrorism strategies and the allocation of resources, focusing on dismantling terrorist networks and preventing future attacks.

Politically, bin Laden's death became a pivotal moment in the 2012 U.S. Presidential election. President Barack Obama, who was in office at the time of the operation, received a significant boost in his public approval ratings. The successful mission showcased his leadership and decisiveness, reinforcing his image as a strong commander-in-chief. This accomplishment became a central theme in his re-election campaign, highlighting his commitment to national security and his administration's achievements in the fight against terrorism.

However, the controversy surrounding bin Laden's death also emerged. Conspiracy theories questioning the authenticity of the operation and raising doubts about bin Laden's actual demise gained traction. These controversies served as a reminder of the challenges in dealing with complex and sensitive operations, fueling debates about transparency and the role of intelligence agencies in the public domain.

Overall, the death of bin Laden not only had a profound impact on the global fight against terrorism but also played a significant role in shaping the political landscape of the United States. It underscored the importance of intelligence gathering, technological advancements, international cooperation, and psychological profiling in counterterrorism operations. The lessons learned from Operation Neptune Spear continue to inform and guide future efforts to combat terrorism and ensure national security.

Chapter 6: The role of technology and surveillance in locating bin Laden

Satellite imagery and aerial surveillance

In the search for Osama bin Laden, the use of satellite imagery and aerial surveillance played a pivotal role in gathering crucial intelligence and providing a comprehensive understanding of the battlefield. This subchapter delves into the significance of these cutting-edge technologies, shedding light on how they helped shape Operation Neptune Spear, the audacious mission that ultimately led to the killing of the world's most wanted terrorist.

Satellite imagery, a powerful tool in the hands of intelligence agencies, allowed for a bird's-eye view of remote areas, including the Pakistan-Afghanistan border region where bin Laden was believed to be hiding. Historians studying the events surrounding Operation Neptune Spear will appreciate the role satellite imagery played in providing accurate and up-to-date information on potential targets. This technology offered a comprehensive overview of the terrain, allowing analysts to identify potential hiding places, observe patterns of movement, and monitor any suspicious activities.

Furthermore, aerial surveillance played an equally indispensable role in the hunt for bin Laden. Unmanned Aerial Vehicles (UAVs), commonly known as drones, offered a unique advantage by combining real-time aerial coverage with the ability to conduct surveillance in hostile environments without endangering human lives. Historians will find it fascinating to explore how these unmanned aircraft provided a constant watchful eye, gathering intelligence on bin Laden's compound and the surrounding areas.

The use of satellite imagery and aerial surveillance also enabled the meticulous planning and execution of Operation Neptune Spear. By analyzing the satellite images and aerial surveillance data, military strategists were able to identify potential escape routes, assess the security measures in place, and anticipate any threats that might arise during the operation. This information proved invaluable in formulating a detailed plan that maximized the chances of success and minimized the risks involved.

Additionally, historians will appreciate the ethical and legal considerations that surrounded the use of satellite imagery and aerial surveillance in this high-stakes operation. The book explores the balance between the need for gathering critical intelligence and the potential implications of violating privacy rights or infringing on national sovereignty.

In conclusion, satellite imagery and aerial surveillance played a vital role in the successful execution of Operation Neptune Spear, leading to the elimination of Osama bin Laden. By providing invaluable intelligence, these technologies allowed for strategic planning, enhanced situational awareness, and minimized risks. Historians studying the intricacies of this historic operation will find this subchapter enlightening as it explores the indispensable role of satellite imagery and aerial surveillance in the hunt for one of the world's most notorious terrorists.

Signal intelligence (SIGINT) collection

Signal intelligence (SIGINT) collection played a crucial role in the successful operation to hunt down and eliminate Osama bin Laden, as detailed in the book "Eyes in the Sky: The Role of Technology and Surveillance in the Hunt for bin Laden." This subchapter explores the significance of SIGINT in Operation Neptune Spear and its impact on intelligence gathering and analysis during the mission.

Throughout the planning and execution of Operation Neptune Spear, the collection of signal intelligence proved to be a game-changer. SIGINT refers to the interception and analysis of electronic communications, including phone calls, emails, and other forms of digital communication. The extensive use of SIGINT allowed intelligence agencies to gain valuable insights into the movements and activities of bin Laden and his associates.

By intercepting and deciphering these communications, analysts were able to piece together a comprehensive picture of bin Laden's network, identify key individuals, and uncover potential vulnerabilities. This intelligence was instrumental in the tactical planning and execution of the operation. The information obtained through SIGINT provided critical details about the compound in Abbottabad, Pakistan, where bin Laden was hiding, including its layout, security measures, and the presence of high-value targets.

Moreover, the Navy SEALs' role in the killing of Osama bin Laden was greatly facilitated by the real-time SIGINT support they received. As they conducted the raid, the SEALs were able to communicate with their command center and access live intelligence feeds, enabling them to adapt their tactics and respond to emerging threats swiftly.

The impact of bin Laden's death on global terrorism cannot be overstated. It dealt a severe blow to al-Qaeda, undermining its leadership and demoralizing its followers. However, the aftermath of bin Laden's death also brought about new challenges. Intelligence agencies had to adapt their strategies and refocus their efforts to address the evolving threat landscape.

The role of technology and surveillance in locating bin Laden cannot be emphasized enough. Advanced satellite imagery, unmanned aerial vehicles (UAVs), and other cutting-edge technologies provided critical intelligence that helped pinpoint bin Laden's whereabouts. The use of these tools in combination with traditional intelligence methods highlighted the importance of integrating different sources of information for successful operations.

In conclusion, the extensive use of SIGINT collection during Operation Neptune Spear was instrumental in the intelligence gathering and analysis that led to the successful elimination of Osama bin Laden. The efficacy of this approach showcased the importance of advanced technology, surveillance, and international cooperation in counterterrorism operations. The lessons learned from this operation continue to shape the way intelligence agencies approach future threats, ensuring a more effective and proactive response to global terrorism.

Cyber surveillance and hacking

Cyber surveillance and hacking played a crucial role in Operation Neptune Spear, the mission that led to the killing of Osama bin Laden. This subchapter explores the significance of cyber intelligence and its impact on the operation's planning, execution, and aftermath.

In the digital age, intelligence gathering relies heavily on cyber surveillance techniques. The hunt for bin Laden was no exception. The book "Eyes in the Sky: The Role of Technology and Surveillance in the Hunt for bin Laden" reveals how advanced technologies and hacking techniques were utilized to track and monitor bin Laden's activities. Through cyber espionage, analysts were able to infiltrate terrorist networks, intercept communications, and gather vital information about bin Laden's whereabouts.

The tactical planning and execution of Operation Neptune Spear heavily incorporated cyber surveillance. The Navy SEALs, who carried out the mission, relied on real-time intelligence gathered through cyber means. This allowed them to accurately assess the situation, identify potential threats, and plan their operation with precision. Cyber surveillance not only provided crucial intelligence but also enhanced the safety and effectiveness of the mission.

The impact of bin Laden's death on global terrorism cannot be overstated. The book explores how cyber surveillance played a pivotal role in disrupting terrorist networks and preventing future attacks. By penetrating the digital infrastructure of these networks, intelligence agencies were able to identify and neutralize high-value targets, thereby crippling their operational capabilities.

The political implications and reactions to bin Laden's killing were significant. The book delves into how cyber surveillance played a role in shaping the political landscape, both domestically and internationally. It examines the reactions of world leaders, the public, and the media, highlighting the role of cyber intelligence in shaping public opinion and understanding of the operation.

Moreover, this subchapter also delves into controversies and conspiracy theories surrounding bin Laden's death. The book examines the various claims and counterclaims, shedding light on the role of cyber surveillance in debunking or supporting these theories.

Finally, the subchapter discusses the lessons learned from Operation Neptune Spear for future counterterrorism operations. It emphasizes the importance of cyber surveillance and hacking as essential tools for intelligence gathering and analysis. It explores how the successful execution of the operation can serve as a blueprint for future missions, highlighting the significance of cyber surveillance as a force multiplier in combating terrorism.

In conclusion, this subchapter provides a comprehensive analysis of the role of cyber surveillance and hacking in Operation Neptune Spear. It highlights the significance of these techniques in intelligence gathering, tactical planning, and execution, as well as their impact on global terrorism, political implications, and future counterterrorism operations.

Utilizing drones in tracking bin Laden

Operation Neptune Spear, the covert mission that led to the killing of the world's most wanted terrorist, Osama bin Laden, was a monumental achievement in the history of counterterrorism. This subchapter explores the pivotal role played by drones in tracking bin Laden and shedding light on his whereabouts.

Unmanned Aerial Vehicles (UAVs), commonly known as drones, revolutionized intelligence gathering and analysis during Operation Neptune Spear. These sophisticated flying machines allowed intelligence agencies to collect vital information without risking the lives of operatives. Equipped with high-resolution cameras and advanced surveillance technology, drones provided a bird's-eye view of the complex landscape where bin Laden was suspected to be hiding.

The tactical planning and execution of Operation Neptune Spear heavily relied on the data and intelligence gathered by drones. Their ability to conduct surveillance from above, undetected, allowed for a comprehensive understanding of bin Laden's compound in Abbottabad, Pakistan. By analyzing drone footage, experts were able to identify patterns of life, assess the compound's defenses, and develop a meticulous plan to infiltrate and neutralize the target.

The Navy SEALs, renowned for their expertise in special operations, played a crucial role in the killing of Osama bin Laden. Drones provided real-time situational awareness, enabling the SEAL team to make informed decisions on the ground. Live feeds from the drones allowed them to navigate through the compound's corridors, neutralize threats, and ultimately locate and eliminate bin Laden.

The impact and aftermath of bin Laden's death on global terrorism cannot be overstated. The successful operation dealt a significant blow to al-Qaeda, both strategically and psychologically. It sent a strong message that no terrorist leader is beyond reach, and it exposed the vulnerabilities of even the most elusive targets.

The political implications and reactions to bin Laden's killing were widespread. The United States and its allies hailed the operation as a victory against terrorism, while some countries expressed concerns about the violation of their sovereignty. The event also sparked debates on the legality and ethics of targeted killings.

Drones, along with other advanced surveillance technologies, played a pivotal role in locating bin Laden. Their ability to conduct long-duration surveillance, gather intelligence, and provide real-time situational awareness was instrumental in the success of Operation Neptune Spear.

Psychological profiling and understanding of bin Laden as a terrorist leader were critical in formulating effective strategies. By analyzing his past actions, speeches, and propaganda, intelligence agencies were able to predict his behavior and make informed decisions during the operation.

International cooperation and intelligence sharing played a vital role in Operation Neptune Spear. The mission's success was the result of a collaborative effort between various intelligence agencies, highlighting the significance of international alliances in combating terrorism.

Controversies and conspiracy theories surrounding bin Laden's death emerged, raising questions about the authenticity of the operation. Some skeptics argued that the entire event was staged, fueling conspiracy theories that persist to this day.

Operation Neptune Spear provided valuable lessons for future counterterrorism operations. It highlighted the importance of technological advancements, international cooperation, and meticulous planning in dealing with high-value targets. The use of drones in tracking bin Laden showcased their potential as indispensable tools in the fight against terrorism.

In conclusion, the utilization of drones in tracking bin Laden was a game-changer in the hunt for the world's most wanted terrorist. These unmanned aerial vehicles provided critical intelligence, aided in tactical planning, and facilitated the successful execution of Operation Neptune Spear. The lessons learned from this operation continue to shape the future of counterterrorism efforts worldwide.

Chapter 7: Psychological profiling and understanding of bin Laden as a terrorist leader

Analyzing bin Laden's background and upbringing

Understanding the background and upbringing of a notorious figure like Osama bin Laden is crucial in comprehending his transformation into a terrorist leader and mastermind. Bin Laden was born into a wealthy and influential Saudi Arabian family in 1957. His father, Mohammed bin Laden, was a successful construction magnate, which allowed Osama to grow up in a privileged environment. However, his family's wealth and status alone cannot solely explain the trajectory of his life.

Bin Laden's formative years were marked by exposure to radical Islamic ideologies. While studying economics and management at King Abdulaziz University in Jeddah, he became influenced by the teachings of prominent Islamist thinkers, particularly Sayyid Qutb. Qutb's writings advocated for a return to a puritanical form of Islam and the establishment of an Islamic state governed by Sharia law.

The Soviet invasion of Afghanistan in 1979 proved to be a turning point for bin Laden. He saw an opportunity to join the fight against the Soviets and actively participated in organizing and funding the resistance movement. This experience solidified his extremist beliefs and provided him with a network of like-minded individuals who would later become crucial to the formation of al-Qaeda.

Bin Laden's time in Afghanistan also allowed him to witness firsthand the power of guerrilla warfare and the potential impact of asymmetrical warfare against a superior military force. These insights would later shape his tactics and strategies as a terrorist leader.

Moreover, bin Laden's experiences during the 1990-1991 Gulf War and his subsequent disillusionment with Saudi Arabia's close ties to the United States further fueled his anti-Western sentiments. These events, coupled with his personal charisma and ability to inspire others, positioned him as a charismatic leader capable of mobilizing individuals from diverse backgrounds to carry out acts of violence in the name of jihad.

Analyzing bin Laden's background and upbringing provides valuable insights into the factors that contributed to his radicalization and the subsequent rise of al-Qaeda. It highlights the importance of understanding the socio-political context in which he operated and sheds light on the motivations and strategies behind his actions.

By examining bin Laden's background, historians can gain a deeper understanding of the complexities involved in counterterrorism efforts. This understanding can inform future intelligence gathering and analysis, tactical planning and execution, and the psychological profiling of potential terrorist leaders. It also underscores the significance of international cooperation and intelligence sharing, as well as the need for effective surveillance and technological advancements to locate and neutralize high-value targets.

Bin Laden's death in 2011 marked a significant milestone in the fight against global terrorism. However, it also sparked controversies and conspiracy theories, which continue to be debated to this day. Lessons learned from Operation Neptune Spear, the operation that led to bin Laden's killing, provide valuable insights for future counterterrorism operations, emphasizing the need for adaptability, intelligence coordination, and the effective utilization of technological advancements.

In conclusion, analyzing bin Laden's background and upbringing provides a foundation for understanding the evolution of a terrorist leader and the factors that shaped his ideology and actions. This knowledge is vital for historians, intelligence professionals, and policymakers alike, as it contributes to a comprehensive understanding of the complexities involved in combating global terrorism.

Ideological motivations driving bin Laden

Subchapter: Ideological Motivations Driving bin Laden

Introduction:

Understanding the ideological motivations that drove Osama bin Laden is crucial to comprehending the mindset of one of the most notorious terrorist leaders in history. This subchapter explores the factors that shaped bin Laden's worldview, delving into his religious beliefs, political ideologies, and deep-seated grievances. By examining these aspects, historians can gain valuable insights into the man who became the face of global terrorism and the catalyst for significant counterterrorism efforts.

Religious Zealotry:

Bin Laden's devotion to radical Islam played a central role in his ideological motivations. Drawing inspiration from the teachings of Sayyid Qutb and Abdullah Azzam, he embraced a fundamentalist interpretation of Islam that advocated for the establishment of a global Caliphate governed by Sharia law. This fundamentalist vision fueled his desire to wage jihad against perceived enemies of Islam, particularly the West, whom he believed were responsible for the degradation of Islamic values.

Anti-American Sentiment:

Bin Laden's animosity towards the United States was deeply rooted in his perception of American imperialism and its support for Israel. His experiences in Afghanistan during the Soviet-Afghan War, where he witnessed the defeat of a superpower, solidified his belief in the vulnerability of the West. The presence of American troops in Saudi Arabia following the Gulf War further fueled his anger, motivating him to orchestrate attacks against American interests worldwide.

Pan-Islamism and Anti-Regime Activism:

In addition to his anti-American stance, bin Laden advocated for the overthrow of Western-backed regimes in the Muslim world. He saw these regimes as puppets serving Western interests, contributing to the suppression of Muslim populations. Bin Laden sought to unite Muslims across national boundaries, rallying them against oppressive regimes and advocating for a return to a puritanical form of Islam.

Conclusion:

Exploring the ideological motivations that drove Osama bin Laden reveals the complex interplay between religious zealotry, anti-American sentiment, and his broader vision for a united Muslim world. Understanding these motivations is essential to grasp the extent of his influence and the gravity of the threat he posed. By delving into bin Laden's ideological beliefs, historians gain a deeper understanding of the man who shaped global terrorism and the challenges faced in countering such radical ideologies in the future.

Leadership and decision-making style

In the subchapter "Leadership and Decision-Making Style" of the book "Eyes in the Sky: The Role of Technology and Surveillance in the Hunt for bin Laden," we delve into the critical factors that shaped the success of Operation Neptune Spear. This section addresses the historians and experts in intelligence gathering and analysis, tactical planning and execution, and counterterrorism operations.

One of the key elements that contributed to the success of Operation Neptune Spear was the exceptional leadership and decision-making style exhibited by the key players involved. The operation required a complex and meticulous approach, and the leaders' ability to make swift and effective decisions was crucial.

At the helm of this operation was a team of highly skilled intelligence professionals, military strategists, and Navy SEALs. Their leadership, characterized by a combination of calmness, adaptability, and assertiveness, was instrumental in the mission's success.

The decision-making style adopted by these leaders was driven by a thorough understanding of the intelligence gathered on Osama bin Laden and the risks associated with the operation. They relied on a combination of technological advancements, surveillance capabilities, and human intelligence to assess the situation and determine the best course of action.

The leaders also fostered a culture of collaboration and information sharing among the different intelligence agencies and international partners involved in Operation Neptune Spear. This approach allowed for a more comprehensive understanding of bin Laden's network and facilitated the coordination of efforts.

Furthermore, the leaders prioritized the safety and well-being of their personnel while ensuring the mission's objectives were met. They demonstrated exceptional crisis management skills, adaptability, and the ability to make critical decisions under immense pressure.

The success of Operation Neptune Spear not only led to the elimination of one of the most notorious terrorist leaders but also had far-reaching implications for global terrorism and counterterrorism strategies. The operation served as a turning point in the fight against terrorism, showcasing the power of technology, surveillance, and international cooperation.

In conclusion, the subchapter "Leadership and Decision-Making Style" highlights the crucial role played by effective leadership and decision-making in the success of Operation Neptune Spear. The leaders' ability to assess intelligence, collaborate with various agencies, and make critical decisions under pressure were key factors in achieving the mission's objectives. This subchapter provides valuable insights and lessons for historians and experts in intelligence gathering, counterterrorism operations, and military strategy for future operations.

Psychological strategies employed by bin Laden

In the pursuit of understanding the mind of one of the world's most notorious terrorists, it is essential to delve into the psychological strategies employed by Osama bin Laden. These strategies shed light on his motivations, decision-making processes, and the tactics he used to manipulate and control his followers.

Bin Laden's psychological profile reveals a complex individual who possessed a deep understanding of human psychology and exploited it to achieve his objectives. One of the key strategies he employed was the use of fear. By leveraging the fear of Western imperialism and the perceived threat to Islam, bin Laden was able to rally support and recruit individuals to his cause. Moreover, he utilized fear as a means to control his followers, ensuring their loyalty through intimidation and coercion.

Another psychological strategy employed by bin Laden was the manipulation of religious ideologies. He skillfully interpreted Islamic teachings to fit his extremist agenda, presenting himself as a champion of Islam and framing his actions as a religious duty. This allowed him to gain legitimacy and support from like-minded individuals who shared his radical interpretation of Islam.

Furthermore, bin Laden utilized propaganda as a powerful tool to shape public opinion and recruit new members. Through the dissemination of carefully crafted messages and videos, he presented himself as a charismatic leader, inspiring admiration and loyalty among his followers. These propaganda efforts were designed to create a sense of unity and purpose, further strengthening his hold on his followers and rallying support for his cause.

In addition to fear, manipulation of religious ideologies, and propaganda, bin Laden employed strategic communication techniques to maintain his influence and control. He utilized encrypted communication channels, ensuring the secrecy of his plans and operations. Moreover, he strategically leaked information to the media, seeking to maintain a public presence and project an image of invincibility.

Understanding these psychological strategies employed by bin Laden is crucial for historians and intelligence analysts. It provides valuable insights into the mindset of a terrorist leader, enabling a more comprehensive understanding of his actions and motivations. By dissecting bin Laden's psychological profile, we can learn important lessons to inform future counterterrorism efforts, enhance intelligence gathering, and develop effective strategies to combat extremist ideologies.

Chapter 8: The role of international cooperation and intelligence sharing in Operation Neptune Spear

Collaborating with foreign intelligence agencies

One of the key elements that contributed to the success of Operation Neptune Spear, the mission that led to the killing of Osama bin Laden, was the collaboration between various foreign intelligence agencies. This subchapter explores the crucial role played by international cooperation and intelligence sharing in the overall success of the operation.

From the early stages of planning to the execution of the mission, intelligence agencies from multiple countries, including the United States, Pakistan, and Saudi Arabia, worked together towards a common goal. Sharing information, resources, and expertise, these agencies formed a formidable alliance that proved instrumental in locating and eliminating one of the world's most wanted terrorists.

The collaboration extended beyond simple information sharing. It involved a deep level of trust and a recognition of the shared threat posed by bin Laden and his global terrorist network. Intelligence agencies had to navigate complex diplomatic and political landscapes to ensure that the mission remained covert and successful.

The significance of international cooperation in Operation Neptune Spear cannot be overstated. It provided vital intelligence on bin Laden's whereabouts, his network, and the security measures surrounding him. Additionally, foreign agencies brought unique perspectives and insights that enriched the overall understanding of the target and his operational capabilities.

However, collaborating with foreign intelligence agencies was not without its challenges. Differing priorities, cultural differences, and the need to protect sensitive information posed obstacles that had to be overcome. The subchapter delves into the difficulties faced by intelligence agencies in establishing trust and ensuring effective communication channels.

Despite these challenges, the successful collaboration between foreign intelligence agencies during Operation Neptune Spear serves as a model for future counterterrorism operations. It highlights the importance of building strong relationships and fostering trust among nations to combat global threats effectively.

This subchapter provides historians and readers interested in intelligence gathering and analysis during Operation Neptune Spear with valuable insights into the complexities of international cooperation. It sheds light on the strategies employed, the lessons learned, and the impact of such collaboration on the outcome of the operation.

In conclusion, the collaboration between foreign intelligence agencies played a crucial role in the success of Operation Neptune Spear. By sharing information, resources, and expertise, these agencies were able to locate and eliminate Osama bin Laden. The subchapter offers a comprehensive exploration of the challenges, achievements, and lessons learned in the realm of international cooperation and intelligence sharing.

Sharing of critical information and resources

Sharing of critical information and resources played a pivotal role in the success of Operation Neptune Spear, the mission that led to the killing of Osama bin Laden. This subchapter delves into the significance of intelligence sharing and its impact on the operation's planning, execution, and aftermath.

The operation required the collaboration of multiple intelligence agencies from around the world, including the CIA, NSA, and ISI. These agencies possessed vital pieces of information that, when combined, provided a comprehensive picture of bin Laden's whereabouts. The sharing of this critical intelligence allowed for the development of a detailed plan to locate and eliminate him.

One crucial aspect of information sharing was the utilization of advanced surveillance technology. Eyes in the sky, such as unmanned aerial vehicles (UAVs) and satellites, provided an unprecedented level of situational awareness. These technological advancements allowed the intelligence community to monitor bin Laden's compound in Abbottabad, Pakistan, without alerting the enemy.

Psychological profiling played a significant role in understanding bin Laden as a terrorist leader. By analyzing his past actions, speeches, and interviews, experts were able to anticipate his behavior and predict his potential hiding places. This information was shared among intelligence agencies, enabling them to narrow down the search and increase the chances of success.

International cooperation was essential in Operation Neptune Spear. The United States collaborated closely with Pakistan, despite the inherent challenges and mistrust. Sharing intelligence and coordinating efforts were crucial to ensure the success of the mission. However, this cooperation was not without controversy, as some questioned Pakistan's level of involvement and potential knowledge of bin Laden's presence.

The aftermath of bin Laden's death had profound global implications. The intelligence gathered from his compound provided valuable insights into al-Qaeda's structure, operations, and future plans. This information was instrumental in disrupting terrorist networks worldwide. However, bin Laden's death also led to an increase in retaliatory attacks by his followers, highlighting the ongoing threat of terrorism.

Operation Neptune Spear taught valuable lessons for future counterterrorism operations. The use of advanced surveillance technology, combined with effective intelligence sharing and international cooperation, proved vital in achieving success. However, controversies and conspiracy theories surrounding bin Laden's death raised questions about transparency and the need for accurate information dissemination in sensitive operations.

In conclusion, the sharing of critical information and resources played a pivotal role in Operation Neptune Spear. This subchapter highlights the importance of intelligence gathering, technological advancements, psychological profiling, international cooperation, and the lessons learned from this historic mission. Understanding these elements provides historians, as well as professionals in intelligence gathering and analysis, tactical planning, and counterterrorism operations, with valuable insights into the complex nature of Operation Neptune Spear and its impact on global security.

Challenges and successes in international cooperation

The successful operation to hunt down and eliminate Osama bin Laden, known as Operation Neptune Spear, was not only a testament to the intelligence, planning, and execution of the mission, but also to the unprecedented level of international cooperation that took place. This chapter delves into the challenges and successes encountered during this crucial aspect of the operation.

International cooperation played a pivotal role in the success of Operation Neptune Spear. The intelligence gathering and analysis during the operation heavily relied on the sharing of information and resources between various intelligence agencies from different countries. This collaboration enabled the pooling of expertise, technology, and surveillance capabilities, resulting in a comprehensive understanding of bin Laden's whereabouts.

However, this level of cooperation was not without challenges. One of the primary obstacles faced was the difficulty of sharing sensitive information among countries with different political agendas and priorities. Trust had to be established, and extensive negotiations and diplomatic efforts were required to ensure a smooth flow of intelligence. The need to balance national security concerns with the imperative to share critical information proved to be a delicate task.

Despite these challenges, international cooperation ultimately triumphed. The success of the operation was a direct result of the coordinated efforts and information sharing between intelligence agencies from multiple nations. The operation showcased the power of collaboration and highlighted the significance of international partnerships in combating global terrorism.

The aftermath of bin Laden's death also demonstrated the impact of international cooperation. The knowledge gained from the operation provided valuable insights into the workings of terrorist networks, enabling countries worldwide to reassess their counterterrorism strategies. Lessons learned from Operation Neptune Spear translated into improved tactics, enhanced intelligence sharing, and more effective international cooperation in future counterterrorism operations.

However, controversies and conspiracy theories surrounding bin Laden's death also emerged. These controversies challenged the credibility of the international cooperation that led to the operation's success. Such skepticism emphasized the need for transparency and accountability in international collaborations, especially during high-stakes operations targeting high-value targets.

In conclusion, the challenges faced during Operation Neptune Spear were numerous, but the successes achieved through international cooperation were undeniable. The operation demonstrated the importance of intelligence sharing, diplomatic negotiations, and trust building among nations. The lessons learned from this historic mission continue to shape and inform future counterterrorism efforts, highlighting the critical role of international cooperation in maintaining global security.

Lessons learned for future joint operations

Operation Neptune Spear, the mission that resulted in the killing of Osama bin Laden, was a pivotal moment in the global war on terror. This operation showcased the importance of various factors such as intelligence gathering, tactical planning, international cooperation, and the use of technology and surveillance. As historians, it is essential to analyze the lessons learned from this operation that can significantly shape future counterterrorism efforts.

First and foremost, the success of Operation Neptune Spear highlighted the critical role of intelligence gathering and analysis. By meticulously piecing together fragments of information from various sources, intelligence agencies were able to pinpoint bin Laden's location with a high degree of accuracy. This emphasizes the need for continued investment in intelligence capabilities, including human intelligence, signals intelligence, and open-source intelligence. Additionally, it underscores the importance of effective analysis and interpretation of gathered intelligence, allowing for timely and decisive actions.

The tactical planning and execution of Operation Neptune Spear demonstrated the value of meticulous planning, training, and coordination among different military branches and units. The mission's success can be attributed to the Navy SEALs' exceptional skills and their ability to adapt to unforeseen challenges. Future joint operations should prioritize comprehensive training, interagency cooperation, and the development of flexible tactics to effectively respond to evolving threats.

The role of technology and surveillance in locating bin Laden cannot be overstated. Advanced surveillance technologies, including unmanned aerial vehicles (UAVs) and satellite imagery, played a crucial role in gathering intelligence and providing real-time situational awareness. The successful utilization of these technologies highlights the need for continued investment in research and development of cutting-edge surveillance capabilities for future operations.

International cooperation and intelligence sharing were key contributors to the success of Operation Neptune Spear. This operation exemplified the effectiveness of collaborative efforts among intelligence agencies from different nations. Lessons learned from this operation emphasize the necessity of fostering strong partnerships and information sharing networks to combat global terrorism collectively.

Finally, Operation Neptune Spear was not without controversies and conspiracy theories surrounding bin Laden's death. Historians must critically examine these controversies to prevent the spread of misinformation and ensure an accurate historical record. This highlights the importance of transparency, accountability, and the need for effective communication strategies during sensitive operations.

In conclusion, Operation Neptune Spear provided invaluable lessons for future joint operations in the fight against terrorism. These lessons underscore the significance of intelligence gathering and analysis, tactical planning and execution, technological advancements, international cooperation, and transparency. By incorporating these lessons into future counterterrorism efforts, nations can enhance their capabilities and ensure the success of future missions.

Chapter 9: Controversies and conspiracy theories surrounding bin Laden's death

The authenticity of bin Laden's death

One of the most significant events in the history of counterterrorism was the killing of Osama bin Laden, the mastermind behind the 9/11 attacks. However, since the announcement of his death, there have been numerous debates and controversies surrounding the authenticity of this event. This subchapter aims to delve into these controversies and shed light on the authenticity of bin Laden's death.

The operation that resulted in bin Laden's demise, known as Operation Neptune Spear, was a meticulously planned and executed mission by the United States Navy SEALs. The intelligence gathering and analysis during this operation played a crucial role in locating bin Laden's hideout in Abbottabad, Pakistan. The role of technology and surveillance in this process cannot be overstated. Advanced surveillance techniques, including satellite imagery, drone technology, and communication intercepts, were instrumental in tracking his movements and confirming his presence in the compound.

The tactical planning and execution of Operation Neptune Spear were executed flawlessly by the Navy SEALs. Their training, expertise, and precision were vital in ensuring the success of the mission. The SEALs' role in the killing of bin Laden was a testament to their bravery and commitment to protecting national security.

However, despite the overwhelming evidence and official confirmation of bin Laden's death, conspiracy theories and controversies emerged. Some skeptics argue that bin Laden's death was staged or that he had already died years earlier. These claims are based on speculations and misinformation, lacking substantial evidence to support them.

The impact and aftermath of bin Laden's death on global terrorism were significant. While his death dealt a severe blow to Al-Qaeda, it did not eradicate the threat entirely. Other terrorist organizations emerged, and the fight against terrorism continued. The political implications and reactions to bin Laden's killing were mixed, with some countries praising the operation as a significant victory while others questioned the legality and sovereignty of the operation.

In conclusion, the authenticity of bin Laden's death is supported by overwhelming evidence and official confirmations. Despite conspiracy theories and controversies, the role of technology, intelligence sharing, and the Navy SEALs' tactical execution in Operation Neptune Spear cannot be undermined. Bin Laden's death had a profound impact on global terrorism, and the lessons learned from this operation continue to shape future counterterrorism efforts.

Allegations of a staged operation

In the subchapter "Allegations of a Staged Operation," we delve into the controversial claims and conspiracy theories surrounding the death of Osama bin Laden during Operation Neptune Spear. While the majority of the world celebrated the successful mission, there are those who question the authenticity of bin Laden's demise.

One of the primary allegations revolves around the notion that the entire operation was a staged event. Skeptics argue that bin Laden had been dead for years, and the United States government used this opportunity to create a narrative that would boost public morale and justify their military presence in the region. These theorists point to the lack of concrete evidence, such as DNA samples or photographs, as proof that bin Laden was indeed killed in the operation.

Another claim suggests that the Navy SEALs' role in the killing of bin Laden was exaggerated. Critics argue that the operation was a carefully crafted propaganda campaign, aimed at showcasing the United States' military prowess. They argue that the SEALs were merely playing a minor role and that the operation was actually carried out by other intelligence agencies or foreign powers.

Additionally, some theorists believe that the U.S. government intentionally withheld vital information about the operation to maintain control over the narrative. They argue that this lack of transparency has fueled conspiracy theories and calls into question the legitimacy of bin Laden's death.

While these allegations and conspiracy theories have garnered attention, it is important to approach them with a critical eye. Historians must carefully evaluate the evidence presented and consider the motives behind these claims. It is essential to separate fact from fiction and rely on credible sources to gain a comprehensive understanding of the events surrounding the operation.

Ultimately, the controversies surrounding bin Laden's death highlight the importance of transparency and accountability in counterterrorism operations. Lessons can be learned from Operation Neptune Spear to ensure that future missions are conducted with the utmost integrity and adherence to international norms. As historians delve into this topic, it is crucial to explore the implications of these allegations on intelligence gathering, military planning, and political decision-making to further our understanding of this historic event.

Speculations on bin Laden's whereabouts and survival

In the aftermath of the devastating 9/11 attacks, the hunt for the mastermind behind the atrocity, Osama bin Laden, became the top priority for intelligence agencies worldwide. As years passed, and bin Laden remained at large, numerous speculations emerged regarding his whereabouts and survival.

Intelligence gathering and analysis during Operation Neptune Spear played a crucial role in narrowing down the potential hiding places of bin Laden. Satellite imagery, intercepted communications, and human intelligence were all utilized to piece together the puzzle. However, the lack of concrete evidence often led to various theories about bin Laden's location.

Some speculated that bin Laden had sought refuge in the mountainous regions of Afghanistan or Pakistan, where he could easily blend in with the local population and take advantage of the rugged terrain. Others believed he had fled to remote areas in Yemen or Somalia, where terrorist networks sympathetic to his cause were known to operate.

The tactical planning and execution of Operation Neptune Spear were focused on capturing or killing bin Laden. The Navy SEALs, renowned for their expertise in special operations, played a pivotal role in this mission. Their training, precision, and ability to adapt to changing circumstances were instrumental in the success of the operation.

The impact and aftermath of bin Laden's death on global terrorism cannot be underestimated. While his demise dealt a severe blow to Al-Qaeda, it also ignited the rise of new extremist groups, such as ISIS. The elimination of bin Laden created a leadership vacuum, resulting in power struggles and splintering within the terrorist network.

The political implications and reactions to bin Laden's killing were diverse. While many celebrated the elimination of a notorious terrorist, others raised concerns over the legality and morality of the operation. Questions arose regarding the violation of Pakistani sovereignty and the potential backlash from extremist sympathizers.

The role of technology and surveillance in locating bin Laden cannot be overstated. Advanced satellite imagery, unmanned aerial vehicles, and sophisticated communication interception systems were all employed to track his movements. The use of facial recognition technology and voice analysis also aided in identifying potential leads.

Psychological profiling and understanding of bin Laden as a terrorist leader were crucial in formulating effective strategies to apprehend him. Experts delved into his ideological beliefs, recruitment tactics, and motivational factors to gain insight into his mindset and decision-making process.

International cooperation and intelligence sharing played a vital role in Operation Neptune Spear. The exchange of information and collaboration between intelligence agencies from different countries significantly enhanced the chances of locating bin Laden. However, controversies arose regarding the extent of Pakistan's knowledge and involvement in harboring bin Laden.

In the aftermath of bin Laden's death, numerous controversies and conspiracy theories surfaced. Some claimed that bin Laden had died years before the operation, while others speculated that the entire mission was a hoax. These theories, although widely debunked, highlight the skepticism and distrust that can surround such high-profile events.

Operation Neptune Spear provided valuable lessons for future counterterrorism operations. It underscored the importance of intelligence sharing, the need for adaptable and specialized forces, and the role of technology in enhancing surveillance capabilities. The operation also highlighted the significance of political considerations and the complex nature of combating terrorism on a global scale.

In conclusion, the speculations on bin Laden's whereabouts and survival during the hunt for him were numerous and varied. The intelligence gathering, tactical planning, and execution of Operation Neptune Spear were crucial in narrowing down his location and ultimately led to his demise. The impact of bin Laden's death on global terrorism, the political implications and reactions, the role of technology and surveillance, and the controversies surrounding his death all contribute to a deeper understanding of this historic event and its lessons for future counterterrorism efforts.

Debunking conspiracy theories through evidence and analysis

The death of Osama bin Laden in 2011 during Operation Neptune Spear sparked numerous controversies and conspiracy theories. However, a comprehensive examination of the available evidence and a careful analysis of the operation's details can effectively debunk these theories.

One of the primary conspiracy theories surrounding bin Laden's death suggests that he is still alive. However, the evidence collected from the operation, including DNA samples, photographs, and testimonies from the Navy SEALs involved, provides overwhelming proof of his demise. The meticulous planning and execution of Operation Neptune Spear also make it highly unlikely that bin Laden could have survived or escaped.

Another conspiracy theory suggests that the United States government had prior knowledge of bin Laden's whereabouts but deliberately delayed his capture for political gain. However, intelligence gathering and analysis during Operation Neptune Spear clearly indicate that locating bin Laden was an arduous and complex process. It required extensive international cooperation and intelligence sharing, as well as advanced technology and surveillance techniques. These factors contributed to the successful operation, dispelling the notion of a deliberate delay.

Furthermore, psychological profiling and understanding of bin Laden as a terrorist leader helped shape the tactical planning and execution of Operation Neptune Spear. The Navy SEALs' role in the killing of bin Laden exemplified their exceptional training, skill, and courage. Their expertise, combined with the use of cutting-edge technology and surveillance, played a crucial role in locating and eliminating the world's most wanted terrorist.

It is crucial to acknowledge that controversies and conspiracy theories often arise in significant events such as this. However, through evidence-based analysis, historians can discern the truth and provide a balanced account of the operation. The impact and aftermath of bin Laden's death on global terrorism, as well as the political implications and reactions it generated, further underscore the significance of this operation.

Ultimately, Operation Neptune Spear offers valuable lessons for future counterterrorism operations. The role of technology and surveillance in locating high-value targets has become increasingly critical. Additionally, international cooperation and intelligence sharing are vital components for success. By studying and understanding the facts surrounding bin Laden's death, historians and professionals in intelligence gathering and analysis can enhance their understanding of counterterrorism efforts and contribute to the prevention of future threats.

Chapter 10: Lessons learned from Operation Neptune Spear for future counterterrorism operations

Evaluating the strengths and weaknesses of the operation

In the pursuit of Osama bin Laden, Operation Neptune Spear was a complex and high-stakes mission that required meticulous planning, precise execution, and the utilization of advanced technology and surveillance techniques. Evaluating the strengths and weaknesses of this operation is crucial to understanding the intricacies and challenges faced by intelligence agencies, military units, and decision-makers involved.

One of the key strengths of Operation Neptune Spear was the exceptional intelligence gathering and analysis capabilities displayed by the participating agencies. The operation relied heavily on the collection and interpretation of actionable intelligence, which allowed for the successful planning and execution of the mission. The ability to gather, analyze, and disseminate intelligence effectively played a pivotal role in locating bin Laden's hideout in Abbottabad, Pakistan.

Tactical planning and execution were other notable strengths of the operation. The Navy SEALs, renowned for their expertise in special operations, were selected for the mission due to their exceptional skills and training. The meticulous planning and attention to detail were evident in the successful infiltration of bin Laden's compound and the subsequent elimination of the target. The operation showcased the SEALs' ability to adapt to changing circumstances and execute a highly sensitive mission flawlessly.

However, the operation also had its weaknesses. One of the primary weaknesses was the reliance on technology and surveillance. While technology played a crucial role in locating bin Laden, it was not infallible. The operation exposed vulnerabilities in the surveillance infrastructure, as bin Laden managed to evade detection for an extended period. This highlighted the need for continuous innovation and improvement in surveillance techniques to adapt to evolving threats.

Another weakness was the controversies and conspiracy theories surrounding bin Laden's death. The operation faced criticism and skepticism, with some questioning the official narrative. It is essential for historians to examine these controversies objectively, to understand the impact they had on public perception and the subsequent global terrorism landscape.

Furthermore, the operation revealed the importance of international cooperation and intelligence sharing. While the operation was carried out by U.S. forces, it was made possible through the collaboration and support of international partners. The successful operation relied on shared intelligence and coordinated efforts, underscoring the significance of international cooperation in counterterrorism operations.

In conclusion, Operation Neptune Spear demonstrated remarkable strengths in intelligence gathering, tactical planning, and execution. However, it also exposed weaknesses in reliance on technology, controversies surrounding bin Laden's death, and the need for continuous international cooperation. Evaluating these strengths and weaknesses is crucial for historians, as it provides valuable insights into the complexities of counterterrorism operations and informs future endeavors in safeguarding global security.

Implementing changes based on lessons learned

In the subchapter titled "Implementing changes based on lessons learned," we delve into the crucial aspect of applying the knowledge gained from Operation Neptune Spear to future counterterrorism operations. This section aims to provide historians, particularly those interested in intelligence gathering and analysis, tactical planning and execution, and the role of technology and surveillance, with valuable insights into the aftermath of bin Laden's death and its impact on global terrorism.

Operation Neptune Spear, the mission that led to the killing of Osama bin Laden, was a turning point in the fight against terrorism. However, it is essential to understand that the success of this operation was not solely due to the efforts of the Navy SEALs involved. Instead, it was a result of meticulous intelligence gathering and analysis, tactical planning, international cooperation, and advanced technology and surveillance.

One of the critical takeaways from Operation Neptune Spear is the importance of psychological profiling and understanding the mindset of a terrorist leader like bin Laden. By comprehending his motivations, methods, and networks, intelligence agencies were able to locate and neutralize him effectively. This knowledge can now be used as a foundation for future counterterrorism operations, enabling intelligence analysts to anticipate the actions of terrorist leaders and disrupt their plans.

Furthermore, the operation highlighted the significance of international cooperation and intelligence sharing. The successful outcome of Neptune Spear was a result of the collaboration between various intelligence agencies and countries. This cooperation not only enhanced the quality of intelligence but also demonstrated the power of unified efforts in combating terrorism on a global scale.

However, Operation Neptune Spear did not come without controversies and conspiracy theories. While the official narrative presents a detailed account of the mission, there have been speculations surrounding the circumstances of bin Laden's death. These controversies, although not directly related to implementing changes, emphasize the importance of transparency and public trust in counterterrorism operations.

In conclusion, Operation Neptune Spear provided valuable lessons that need to be implemented in future counterterrorism operations. The understanding of psychological profiling, the role of international cooperation, and the significance of advanced technology and surveillance should guide intelligence agencies in their pursuit of combating terrorism effectively. Moreover, it is essential for governments to address controversies and conspiracy theories surrounding such operations, as transparency and public trust are vital in this fight against global terrorism. By incorporating these lessons learned, we can enhance our capabilities and stay one step ahead in the ongoing battle against terrorism.

Enhancing intelligence gathering and analysis capabilities

In the pursuit of Osama bin Laden, the United States faced numerous challenges that required the enhancement of intelligence gathering and analysis capabilities. Operation Neptune Spear, the mission that ultimately led to the demise of the world's most wanted terrorist, relied heavily on the ability to collect and interpret intelligence accurately.

The success of the operation was largely attributed to the advancements in technology and surveillance techniques. The book "Eyes in the Sky: The Role of Technology and Surveillance in the Hunt for bin Laden" delves into the innovative methods employed by intelligence agencies to locate and track bin Laden.

Sophisticated satellite imagery, unmanned aerial vehicles (UAVs), and other cutting-edge surveillance technologies played a crucial role in the identification of bin Laden's compound in Abbottabad, Pakistan. The book explores the specific tools and strategies used to gather intelligence and analyze it effectively, shedding light on the meticulous planning and execution of Operation Neptune Spear.

Intelligence gathering and analysis during Operation Neptune Spear were not without their challenges. The book delves into the complexities faced by intelligence agencies, such as the difficulty of infiltrating bin Laden's inner circle and the reliance on human intelligence sources. It also highlights the importance of psychological profiling and understanding bin Laden as a terrorist leader, providing valuable insights into his mindset and decision-making processes.

International cooperation and intelligence sharing played a vital role in the success of Operation Neptune Spear. The book examines the collaborative efforts of intelligence agencies from around the world, showcasing how the sharing of information and resources contributed to the eventual elimination of bin Laden.

However, the aftermath of bin Laden's death brought about various controversies and conspiracy theories. The book uncovers these controversies and explores their impact on public perception and the future of counterterrorism operations. It also delves into the political implications and reactions to bin Laden's killing, providing historians with a comprehensive understanding of the global response.

By analyzing the lessons learned from Operation Neptune Spear, this subchapter provides valuable insights for future counterterrorism operations. It emphasizes the importance of enhancing intelligence gathering and analysis capabilities, fostering international cooperation, and leveraging technology and surveillance in the ongoing fight against global terrorism.

For historians and individuals interested in intelligence gathering and analysis, this subchapter provides an in-depth exploration of the role played by these capabilities during Operation Neptune Spear and the significance of their enhancement in the pursuit of bin Laden and future counterterrorism efforts.

Adapting tactics and strategies for evolving terrorist threats

In the subchapter, "Adapting Tactics and Strategies for Evolving Terrorist Threats," we delve into the crucial aspect of counterterrorism operations – the ability to adapt and evolve in the face of ever-changing threats. The successful execution of Operation Neptune Spear, which led to the elimination of Osama bin Laden, serves as a prime example of the importance of adaptive tactics and strategies.

During Operation Neptune Spear, intelligence gathering and analysis played a pivotal role in identifying and locating bin Laden. Historians will find this section particularly intriguing as it explores the intricate details of how multiple intelligence agencies cooperated, shared information, and employed cutting-edge technology and surveillance systems to track down the world's most wanted terrorist. The role of technology and surveillance was paramount in locating the elusive bin Laden, and this subchapter offers a comprehensive analysis of the various tools and techniques used.

Tactical planning and execution are equally crucial to the success of any counterterrorism operation. This section provides historians with a detailed account of how Navy SEALs meticulously planned and executed the raid on bin Laden's compound in Abbottabad, Pakistan. It explores the unique challenges they faced, the strategies employed to overcome them, and the lessons learned that can be applied to future operations.

The subchapter also sheds light on the Navy SEALs' exceptional role in the killing of Osama bin Laden. By studying their training, tactics, and execution, historians can gain a deeper understanding of the elite forces entrusted with carrying out such high-profile missions.

Furthermore, the impact and aftermath of bin Laden's death on global terrorism are discussed. This includes an examination of the political implications and reactions from various nations, as well as an exploration of the controversies and conspiracy theories that emerged surrounding bin Laden's death.

Lessons learned from Operation Neptune Spear are invaluable for future counterterrorism operations. Historians will appreciate the analysis of how this operation revolutionized intelligence gathering, tactical planning, and execution. The subchapter also emphasizes the importance of international cooperation and intelligence sharing, highlighting the role of various nations in bringing down bin Laden.

In conclusion, "Adapting Tactics and Strategies for Evolving Terrorist Threats" offers historians a comprehensive look into the multifaceted aspects of Operation Neptune Spear. From intelligence gathering and tactical planning to the role of technology and the impact on global terrorism, this subchapter provides valuable insights and lessons that can be applied in future counterterrorism operations.